HISTORY QUIC

Stories of An

By David Oakden

Illustrated by Gillian Marklew

ANGLIA *young* BOOKS

First published in 1995
by Anglia Young Books
Durhams Farmhouse
Ickleton
Saffron Walden, Essex CB10 1SR

Illustrations by Gillian Marklew

British Library Cataloguing-in-Publication Data
A catalogue record for this book is available from the British Library

ISBN 1 871173 41 8

Typeset in Sassoon Primary by Goodfellow & Egan, Cambridge and printed in Great Britain by Ashford Press, Curdridge, Southampton

CONTENTS

THE FIRST MARATHON
490 BC

Lem was a Greek soldier from the city of Athens. All the young men of Athens had to go in the army for two years. Lem was looking forward to getting home again.

Lem's unit was at a place called <u>Marathon</u>. Marathon was near the sea, about twenty five miles from

Athens. Lem had his own armour, made of <u>bronze</u>. He had a <u>breastplate</u>, bronze shields on his legs and a fine helmet.

The Greek soldiers were very good fighters. They were known as <u>hoplites</u>. They trained hard, ran fast and fought bravely. They were not afraid of any army anywhere, except for the <u>Persian</u> army.

The Persian army was large and its soldiers were good fighters. The people of Persia hated the people of Athens.

One morning Lem and his friend Demos sat cleaning their armour. 'I think we could beat the Persians,' said Lem. 'Our armour is light and we can run fast. The Persians are slow!'

Demos polished his spear. 'Yes,' he said. 'But remember the Persian horses. Persians on horses are very fast. They could cut us to pieces.'

'I'm glad my time in the army is nearly over,' said Lem. 'In a few weeks I shall be twenty. Then I can go back home to Athens.'

Demos lifted his sword in the air. 'Haven't you heard the news, Lem?' he said. 'The war has started again. The Persian army is on its way here to attack us.'

Lem jumped to his feet. 'That's terrible!' he said. 'Persia is such a large country and Athens is so small. Shall we get help from other people?'

'The Spartans said they would help,' said Demos. 'A man called Pheidippides has run with a message to them.'

'Sparta?' said Lem. 'That's a hundred and fifty miles away. They will take a long time to get here.'

Some days later, Lem and Demos woke up to hear a trumpet. 'What's that?' said Lem, sitting up.

'The Persians are here!' said Demos. 'Quick, get your armour on.'

There were ships down by the shore. The Persian army had landed! They had bows and swords and there were thousands of men on horseback.

Lem pointed to the men on horseback. 'The Persian <u>cavalry</u>,' he said with a shudder. 'We shall all be killed.'

The small Greek army waited. They had about nine thousand men. The Persians had many more.

Three days went by and still the Persian army did not attack. Then a spy came with some news. 'The Persian cavalry has ridden north,' he said. 'They are going to come from behind and drive us into the sea.'

'We must attack the rest of the Persian army now, while the cavalry is away,' said the Greek generals. 'Our men are rested. They are fit. The Persians have had a sea voyage. The sooner we attack the better.'

Trumpets sounded, orders were given and the Greek hoplites moved to attack. They ran forward steadily.

Arrows flew through the air. One hit Demos on the head but his helmet saved him. Another grazed Lem's arm. He wrapped a cloth round it and ran on.

Then they were in the middle of the battle. The noise was terrible. Men were screaming and swords and spears were clashing against armour. It was hand-to-hand fighting to the death.

The Persians fought hard, but the Greeks were fit and strong.

Lem cut down a Persian soldier just as he was fitting an arrow to his bow. Then he came face to face with another soldier. The Persian struck at Lem with his spear.

Lem stepped sideways. His sword hit the Persian's armour and slid off. Then the Persian crashed his spear against Lem's helmet. Lem fell to the ground, his ears ringing.

As he fell he twisted. He was just in time. The Persian's spear thudded into the ground just where he had been lying. Lem gasped and looked up. The Persian was standing over him, grinning, his sword raised.

'Die, dog!' snarled the Persian. The sword came down. But Lem rolled sideways again and thrust upwards with his own sword. The point went

into the Persian's neck and with a groan the man fell on top of him.

Lem heaved the body off and got to his feet, just as Demos staggered up. He was covered in blood and his helmet had gone. 'I'm finished,' he groaned. 'I have a spear in my leg.' He collapsed on the ground.

Lem could feel blood running down his face from a cut above his eye. He took hold of Demos and pulled him into some bushes. The spear had gone into the back of his leg and broken off. The point was still in there, in the fleshy part.

'Lie still!' said Lem. He took hold of the broken spear and pulled. It came, and blood poured out. Lem tore a piece off his tunic and bound up the wound. He gave Demos his leather flask of wine. 'Stay there,' he ordered. 'When the battle is over I will come for you.'

For hours the battle went on. Then suddenly somebody shouted, 'They are running!'

And they were! The Persians were running for their boats.

The news spread and a great cheer went up. The Greek army charged after them, running fast and killing as they went.

As they got close to the beaches, the Persian cavalry came riding back, but they were too late. The Greeks dragged them off their horses and killed or captured them. The Battle of Marathon was over and the mighty Persian army had been beaten.

Lem went and found Demos so that his wound could be dressed. Lem got someone to bind his own wounds. He was very tired. He had fought so hard.

6,400 Persians died. The Greeks only lost 192. It had been a great victory. The men stood round panting. But then the general said, 'We must send the good news to Athens. Who will run there?'

'Let me go, general,' said Lem.

'Yes,' said the general. 'I have heard how you saved your friend. You fought well. You are the one to go.'

The troops cheered. Lem threw down his armour and set off at once. Athens was about twenty-five miles away. He was tired and feeling faint from his wounds. But he knew that he had to get there.

He ran and ran. On the way he shouted the news to villages. Men and women cheered the blood-stained soldier.

The moon was rising as Lem ran into the centre of Athens and collapsed. He felt strong arms lifting him up and a cup of wine was put to his lips.

'What news?' said a voice.

'Great news,' said Lem faintly. 'The Persian army has been beaten.

Thousands of them are dead and the rest have fled. Our army has won a great victory at Marathon.'

People started to cheer, but Lem lay back. His head rested on the steps of the temple. Gradually his life faded from him.

Lem died a hero. That was over 2500 years ago, but even to this day we remember his famous run from Marathon to Athens. The Olympic Games are held every four years and one race is run over twenty-six miles. That race is known as the Marathon.

GLOSSARY

breastplate
armour worn on the chest

bronze
metal made out of tin and copper

cavalry
soldiers on horseback

hoplite
a Greek soldier. All Greek men had to serve in the army
for two years.

Marathon
a place about 25 miles North-East of Athens

Persia
a large country, now called Iran.

Sparta
a Greek state 150 miles North of Marathon

HISTORICAL BACKGROUND for
THE FIRST MARATHON

Athens had no full-time army. At the age of 18, every young man began military training and served for two years.

In 490 BC Greece was at war with Persia. When Persia attacked, a man called Pheidippides was sent with a message to Sparta asking for help. However, the Spartans refused to help until the moon was full. By then the battle was all over.

If the Persian cavalry had charged at once, they would have won. However, they were tired after the sea journey, and also the Greeks had made banks of earth to stop the horses. So the cavalry rode North. When they were out of the way the

Greeks attacked. The result was a brilliant victory.

The name of the man who ran from Marathon to Athens is not known. Some people think it was Pheidippides, the man who had run to Sparta. But most accounts of the legend just say that the man who ran from Marathon to Athens was a Greek soldier.

Marathon is about 25 miles from Athens, but the modern Marathon race is run over a distance of 26 miles and 385 yards (42.195 km). This is because, when the Olympic Games were held in London in 1908, King Edward VII said that the race must start at his castle at Windsor and finish in front of the royal box at the White City stadium in London.

THE SLAVE AND THE WOLF
448 BC

Kara was a slave. He lived in Athens and he worked for an important man called Silves. Kara had been born a slave. Now he was a man, tall and very strong, but he was still a slave.

Every day Kara took his master's son to school. His master's son was called Hilos. Hilos was nine years old and did not like school.

'How can I learn all these letters?' he grumbled. He showed Kara a board covered in wax. Words were scratched in the wax.

'I can't read,' said Kara. 'What does it say?'

Hilos read it to him. 'It says <u>Hercules</u> was a strong man,' said Hilos. He went on: 'Our teacher told us that Hercules killed two snakes when he was only a baby. He strangled them.'

Kara liked that story. 'I want to be like Hercules,' he said. 'I want to be a wrestler.'

When Hilos got home, his father Silves and his mother Metis were waiting. 'Get ready for a journey,' said Silves. 'We are going to <u>Delphi</u>.'

'Delphi?' said Hilos. 'That is where the god <u>Apollo</u> speaks to people, isn't it? Why are we going there?'

'Your mother has a question to ask Apollo,' said Silves. 'She has had a dream about your sister Petra. She thinks that Petra is in trouble.

'Can we go to see Petra?' asked Hilos.

Silves shook his head. 'She lives in the town of <u>Olympia</u>. That is 170 miles away, over the mountains. Now no more questions. Tell Kara to get the horses.'

The family rode on three horses, but Kara the slave walked. He led two pack-horses with clothes, food and weapons.

At last they reached Delphi. There were hundreds of people there, all wanting help from the gods. Silves went to the temple and made offerings to Apollo. He gave money and he also gave a goat. A priestess sprinkled the goat with water.

'Look,' said Hilos. 'The goat is shivering!'

'That is a good sign,' said the priestess. 'Follow me.'

They went down a dark tunnel to a room under the ground. The priestess went behind a curtain. Hilos was frightened and held his father's hand.

A voice came from behind the curtain. It sounded hollow and strange. 'What is your question?' asked the voice.

Metis said, 'My daughter lives in Olympia. I had a dream about her. Is she well or is she sick?'

There was no answer for a time. Then the voice said, 'The moon rises and the moon falls – but the gods smile.'

'What does that mean?' asked Metis. 'That is all,' said the voice. 'Apollo has spoken.'

Silves and Metis did not know what to do. Apollo had spoken but they could not understand what he had said.

Outside the temple a new moon was shining in the dark sky. Kara was still thinking about Hercules. 'How far is it to Olympia from here?' he said to Hilos.

Hilos said, 'It's a long way. If we started now, that new moon would be full before we got there.'

Silves was close by. 'That's it!' he shouted. 'That's what the message means. The god Apollo is talking about how long it takes to make a journey. If we want to see Petra in Olympia, it will take us until the moon is full. But the gods will smile on us if we go.'

Metis said, 'Oh dear, Olympia is so far away. Are you sure? This year is the year of the Games. Everything will be expensive. There will be robbers and wolves in the mountains.'

Kara was excited. 'Please let us go to Olympia,' he said. 'I will look after you on the way. When we get there I can wrestle at the Games. I want to be like Hercules.'

'Be quiet!' snapped Silves. 'The Olympic Games are not for slaves.' He turned to his wife. 'We will go to Olympia. It will stop you worrying about Petra.'

They set off. The first night they slept at an inn, but in the morning Silves woke up scratching himself.

'Bed-bugs!' he grumbled. 'No more inns. From now on we sleep at the roadside.'

But Metis would not do that. 'What about robbers and wolves?' she said. 'We shall all wake up dead!'

So every night they slept at an inn, but Kara had to search the beds for bugs before Silves would get in.

At last they were near to Olympia. 'There is no inn,' said Silves, 'We must sleep on the side of the road.'

In the night they heard a loud howling noise. It was a wolf. Everyone woke up and Silves got out his sword.

'Wolves!' he said, and at that very moment they heard Metis scream. A wolf had smelt food in her bag. It was attacking her as she lay on the ground. In the moonlight they could see its snarling jaws.

Silves ran towards it. He did not want to use his sword in case he hurt his wife, but Kara the slave did not wait. He threw himself at the wolf and wrestled with it. He grabbed it by the throat and rolled in onto its back.

The wolf snarled and snapped its yellow teeth. Its sharp claws dug into Kara's arms. The wolf and the slave rolled over and over. Silves still could not use his sword.

'Help Kara, Father,' shouted Hilos.

'He will be killed. Look at the blood on his arms!'

But then there was a terrible howl of pain. The wolf's body jerked and lay still. Kara had broken its neck.

Silves and Metis ran to the slave. Metis bandaged his wounds with a clean cloth. Then Silves said, 'Kara, you saved my wife's life. I am making you a free man. You are a slave no longer.'

'Can he wrestle at the Olympic Games?' said Hilos.

Silves smiled. 'Yes,' he said. 'I will see to it.'

When they got to Olympia, Silves asked about Petra. There was good news. She was safe and well, living in a good house with her husband. She was very happy to see them, and she had a surprise for them.

'Come with me,' she said. She led them into the cool garden. There, in a wooden cot, lay a baby boy. 'His name is Silves,' she said. 'Like his grandfather.'

Next day was the first day of the Olympic Games, so they all went to the stadium. This was a flat, open space outside the town. All round it was a bank where people sat to watch the games.

Trumpets blew and the games started. There were a lot of speeches and prayers to the gods. 'I wish they would get on with the sports,' said Hilos.

The next two days were more exciting. There were chariot races and running races.

Then at last it was the day for the wrestling. Kara stripped and fought with man after man. He was only thrown once, and soon he had beaten everybody. Hilos cheered until he lost his voice.

On the last day all the winners paraded in front of the crowd. The chief judge put crowns of <u>olive</u> leaves on the winners' heads. Trumpets blew and the crowd cheered. Kara was an Olympic champion.

'Well done, Kara,' said Silves. 'I hope you will come home with us and still be our servant. Then in four years' time, we will come back.'

'Yes,' said Kara. 'Next time I will go in for the <u>pentathlon</u>. That means I shall have to wrestle again. But I will also have to run, jump, throw the <u>javelin</u> and hurl the <u>discus</u>. Five events.'

'Good idea!' said Hilos. 'If you win the Pentathlon, Father will pay for a statue of you to be put in the stadium. That is the custom.'

Kara smiled. 'Well then,' he said, 'I must do some training. I wonder if there will be any more wolves on the way home!'

GLOSSARY

Apollo
the Greek god of light, music and healing

bed-bug
an insect which lives in beds and bites people

Delphi
city with a temple to Apollo

discus
a round metal plate: the winner of the discus-hurling event
was the one who threw the discus the furthest

Hercules
Greek hero, famous for his strength

javelin
a throwing spear

olive
a tree with glossy leaves

Olympia
The Olympic Games were held at Olympia every four
years from 776 BC until AD 394. Women were not allowed
to take part

pentathlon
five sports: running, jumping, wrestling, throwing the javelin,
throwing the discus

stadium
an open space for games and races

HISTORICAL BACKGROUND for
THE SLAVE AND THE WOLF

The Ancient Greeks believed that the gods would help them by answering their questions. One way to do this was to go to Apollo's Temple in the city of Delphi. At the temple there were priests, who made sacrifices for the people. The priests knew, from the way the sacrifice burned, what the gods wanted the people to do. However, the answers were often like riddles, very difficult to understand.

Long journeys were not easy in 448 BC. Roads were rough and mountain tracks were dangerous.

The Olympic Games were held every four years in honour of the god Zeus. Wrestling was very popular and went on until one man gave in. Biting and gouging out eyes were fouls! Statues of pentathlon winners, who were the greatest athletes, were put up in the stadium.

The Games lasted 5 days. Day 5 was given over to prize-giving and feasting.

THE WEDDING GIFT
400 BC

Creon stood in his stall in the Street
of the Potters. All round him were
pots which he had made – small
pots and large pots – tall pots for
wine and fat jars for olives, vases
for flowers and clay bins for flour.
Creon had made them all. Creon
was the best potter in Athens, but
today he looked worried.

'What's the matter, Father?' asked Niki his daughter. She was there with her twin sister Nenna.

Creon said, 'It is Helen, my richest customer. She buys a lot of my pots. Her son is getting married to the daughter of a very important man. She wants to give them a special wine jar for a wedding present.'

'That is good,' said Niki.

'Yes. But she cannot make up her mind about the picture on the pot. I said that there could be a ship, perhaps, or the goddess of love, or bunches of grapes.'

'All good ideas,' said Nenna.

'She does not think so,' said Creon. 'She wants me to make the pot first and then show it to her. But if I do that, she may not like it. Then she will tell people that I am no good. Look, here she comes now.'

A big lady came down the street, followed by two slaves. She was wearing a long dress called a peplos. A sash was round her waist and her dark, curly hair was held back by a jewelled ribbon.

'Out of the way, you two,' said Creon to the twins.

The lady stopped. One of the slaves had a big dog on a lead. This was Arrow, Helen's hunting dog. He was brown with long legs and shaggy hair.

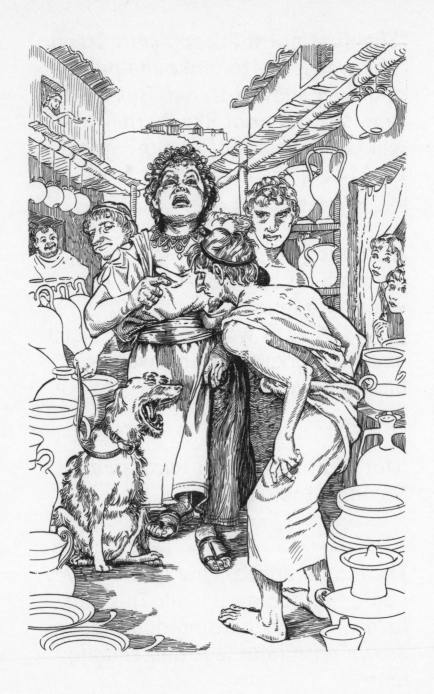

Creon bowed. Helen said, 'Have you made my pot? If you cannot make it, I shall go to another potter.'

That night Niki and Nenna sat in their house. Their mother was feeding the baby. Creon was making more pots.

Niki was using a <u>spindle</u> to spin wool into <u>yarn</u>. Nenna was weaving the yarn on her <u>loom</u>. They were working to make a new blanket for the baby's cot.

'I need more wool,' said Niki. 'Jason the shepherd has a <u>fleece</u> that I can have. Come with me, Nenna.'

They set off. It was getting dark, but there was a moon. They walked

round the great hill of the <u>Acropolis</u>.
Soon they came to part of the town
where the houses were poor and the
streets were dirty.

'There's a nasty smell,' said Nenna.

'It's that broken drain,' said Niki.
'Look.'

The drains in Athens ran under the
streets. They carried dirty water
away to the sea.

The bad smell was coming from a
deep hole in the road. At the bottom
they could see dirty water in the
drain.

'Let's go,' said Nenna. 'It makes me
feel sick.'

They walked on. But then they heard dogs barking. Two dogs came racing past. A small dog was chasing a big brown dog with shaggy hair.

The dogs stopped at the hole in the road. The small dog sank its teeth into the big dog's leg. The big dog yelped and fell backwards into the drain. The small dog ran off.

'That's Arrow, Helen's dog,' said Niki.

The dog was lying in the dirty water at the bottom of the drain. It was lying very still.

Niki lay down in the mud and reached down. She could just touch the dog's back.

'Hold my legs,' she said to Nenna.

'Don't fall in,' said Nenna. 'The water is filthy. It will make you ill.'

'That's why we must get the dog out,' said her sister.

Arrow was moving. Niki grabbed his back leg and heaved. Nenna heaved as well. The dog came out and all three tumbled in the mud.

Arrow was whining. He could not walk. 'We must take him home,' said Niki. 'Father will know what to do.'

When they got home Creon was worried. 'That's Helen's dog,' he said. 'Look at the blood. If he dies Helen will blame us.'

They took the dog out to the yard. Niki got a bowl of warm water and gently bathed the bites. Creon said, 'I will ask Pallos, the doctor, what to do.'

'Can you help this poor dog?' Creon said to Pallos.

Pallos looked at Arrow. 'I cure people, not dogs,' he grumbled. 'But I will tell you what to do. First, cut off all the hair round the bites. Wash off the blood. Then put this ointment on. Put this powder in water and give it to the animal to drink. It will make the dog sleep for twelve hours.' It was now very late, but Creon went round to Helen's house with the news. She rushed down to see Arrow. He had taken the powder and was asleep, on a rug.

'He's dead!' she screamed. 'What have you done? And look at his beautiful coat. It's all cut away in patches. You stupid man. I will never buy another pot from you. You need not make the wedding pot!'

Creon tried to explain, but she did not listen. Her slave picked Arrow up and they left.

Creon could not believe his bad luck. He started shouting at everybody. 'I am ruined,' he yelled. 'And all because of a dog.' He stormed off to bed.

The twins were left alone. Arrow's hair was lying in a heap. Niki said, 'I have an idea. I think we can make things better. This is what we are going to do.'

Niki's plan took all night, but by morning the girls had finished.

Later that day Creon was at his stall. Soon Helen came. Two slaves were carrying Arrow in a basket.

'Now then,' said Helen. 'I want to know just how my poor dog got injured. You said it was something to do with your girls. They must be punished.'

Niki and Nenna came out from the back of the stall. They told Helen what had happened.

'Hm,' said Helen. 'That might be true. But there was no need to cut Arrow's hair off like that.'

'Yes there was,' said Niki. 'The dirty hair would stop the wound getting better. Arrow would have died.'

Nenna said, 'Out of bad comes good. Look.' She showed Helen a sash and a hair-band.

'They are beautiful,' said Helen. 'But what have they got to do with Arrow?'

'They are made from Arrow's hair,' said Nenna. 'Niki mixed it with wool and spun it. Then I wove it. They are presents for you.'

Helen started to cry. She said, 'Thank you. I shall wear the sash and the hairband tonight. I will show them to all my friends. They will want you to do the same for them and their pets. They will pay well.'

She turned to Creon. 'I have changed my mind about the pot,' she said. 'I don't want one. I want two. One pot must show your daughter spinning the yarn. The other must show her sister weaving it.'

Creon bowed. 'Thank you,' he said. 'That will look good. And on the other side of each pot I will paint Arrow hunting. What splendid wedding presents they will make.'

GLOSSARY

<u>aqueduct</u>
a canal for carrying water, often built high on stone or iron
pillars

<u>Acropolis</u>
the highest part of Athens where the most important
buildings were

<u>fleece</u>
the raw wool from a sheep

<u>loom</u>
a frame for weaving thread into cloth

<u>peplos</u>
a long dress worn by Greek ladies

<u>spindle</u>
a wooden pin used for twisting wool into a thread

<u>yarn</u>
thread made from twisted wool

HISTORICAL NOTES for THE WEDDING GIFT

In 400 BC Athens was a rich state with many fine buildings. The city was built round the hill of the Acropolis. On that hill were temples and other town buildings. At the foot of the hill lived the poorer people.

Athens had a good system for bringing fresh water to the town and taking away the waste. Stone drains ran under the streets and large <u>aqueducts</u> carried water to the city.

Greek ladies wore a dress made from one piece of material, wound round them. It was called a peplos. They wore a sash round their waists and their hair was held back by a band of cloth.

Most of the jugs and cooking-pots used in Greek houses were made of pottery. The market had very many stalls where pots were sold. The Greeks liked to paint their pots with scenes of people and animals.